Multilateral Minds

OrangeBooks Publication

1st Floor, Rajhans Arcade, Mall Road, Kohka, Bhilai, Chhattisgarh 490020

Website: **www.orangebooks.in**

© Copyright, 2024, Author

All rights reserved. No part of this book may be reproduced, stored in a retrieval system, or transmitted, in any form by any means, electronic, mechanical, magnetic, optical, chemical, manual, photocopying, recording or otherwise, without the prior written consent of its writer.

First Edition, 2024

ISBN: 978-93-6554-940-9

Jack of all trades is master of none, but...

Multilateral Minds

Murali Karthik

OrangeBooks Publication
www.orangebooks.in

For

My Parents, Teachers, Mentors

And All the Well-Wishers.

Jack of all trades master of none, but better than master of one

"To be a successful multitalented person in the modern day, you ought to channelize your talents"

-Dr. Prem Jagyasi

Introduction

◇――――― ―――――◇

Who is Murali Karthik?

I spent my childhood majorly with myself. I have a sister with me and all the things around me were working as same as everyone's life in a clockwise direction. Wish spending time myself all the time without discovering it resulted compound effect. Anything that you do for a long time with give you hefty outcome, its anything. It might be investing, academics, sports and many others. But in my case its managing multiple interests. This book of mine will give you a clever understanding about how am I able to diversify from head to tail without leaving a bit.

I am Murali Karthik, let me tell you what I do. Currently while writing this book. I am 17-Year-Old, Undergrad in BBA, owning a Social Media Marketing & Advertising Agency, Content Creator, Astrologer, Research Associate, Equity Investor, Derivatives Trader, Lyricist, and now I am an Author.

You must be wondering how a 17-year-old kid is able to do these things. This book will tell you.

I am either encouraged to do more and think more or I do often get suggestions to not continue this mind. This is harmful for you and your career. I had been told this, to be cautious and take wise decisions and not to eat whatever comes in your hand.

Instead replying each one I thought to write this book. This book will give you a vivid description on how does my mind work, things work, and how do I run it?

Multilateral Minds, this book is a deep dive into the multilateral world. It has very less chapters and watch having its own valid answer.

It's not a long book. You're welcome. Most readers don't end their book due to unnecessary exaggeration. Here I present a quickie that you can complete with an ease.

Here we go.

Content

Introduction _____ vi

1. Jack of All Trades Master of None _____ 1

2. Multilateral > Unilateral _____ 8

3. Diversify or Die! _____ 16

4. Don't Put All Your Eggs in One Basket _____ 23

5. Pick Passive _____ 33

6. Mind Management _____ 37

1
Jack of All Trades Master of None

Jack of All Trades Master of None

Jack of all trades, master of none" could serve as a poignant reminder of the complex nature of expertise. This shows the versatility of individuals who dabble in various skills, yet it also highlights the challenge of achieving mastery in any one pursuit.

It suggests that while breadth of knowledge can be valuable, depth is often sacrificed in the pursuit of diverse interests. In a world that celebrates specialization, this age-old saying prompts reflection on the balance between exploration and mastery in our personal and professional journeys.

Jack of all trades, master of none is a famous saying. Some people tend to do everything in their life but end up doing something else in their life. Starting with something, thinking of something and doing something. I am a perfect example of that.

I have a flickering mindset that just doesn't sit in a place. My mind works all the time not efficiently but unnecessarily many times.

Due to the extensive information load, I cannot focus on important things either. I am lost in thoughts the majority of the time. I live in the past, present, and future confusing my brain as well as yours.

Living in the past makes me depressed, living in the future makes me anxious, and living in the present moment is difficult. But I am trying to opt for the third option, living in the present moment and having a little thought on the past and future.

Sustainable Development it is, ha-ha. In this book, I will explain exactly what kind of person I am and belong to the multilateral mindset.

Artists and Poets are lost in their worlds-imagination and overthinking lead to Creativity and Art. This helped me even. This is an excuse you might think but I believe it firmly.

I am not a topper in my school. I was an average and below-average student in kindergarten, primary and secondary school. I was the same, I was experimental with my life but never understood how to balance everything.

Why did this happen? Due to lack of concentration in the class. I was lost all the time in my world. I used to write stories ignoring studies during my primary school, I used to write poems, songs, and many more during secondary school. When I completed high school, I mastered management within no time. I became serious with my work.

I accelerated my time, energy, money, and mind management. I was not interested in academics all the time. I was interested in extra and co-curricular activities. I used to dance, sing, write, talk, create, and many more. Soon people started naming me "MULTITALENTED".

That gave me more boost and encouragement to excel in as many subjects as possible. I play tennis, cricket, swimming and many more. I touched almost many topics. Having numerous works with me I lack focus which is the most important thing in life.

I cannot sit and focus on one thing properly for a long time. My parents were supportive and encouraging, which gave me another kick.

In today's fast-paced world, where everybody is busy with their worlds building wealth, winning bread, fostering their children, and fulfilling their needs and wants. In such a busy world people don't getthe appropriate time, energy, and money to try out different skills.

People pick one job or career path which is either chosen by them, by their surroundings like family and friends, or by following a blind route made by a blind person long years ago. In such a world where specialization is often lauded as the path to success, the phrase "Jack of all trades, master of none" resonates with both admiration and caution.

It speaks to the allure of versatility, acknowledging the allure of individuals who possess a wide array of skills and knowledge.

Some people admired me for my achievements and encouraged me to move forward, as many of them didn't take it seriously and called it childishness which will fade out in no time and some people cautioned me several times to not diversify and put my legs in different boats.

However, it also serves as a gentle warning, reminding us of the potential pitfalls of spreading oneself too thin. While the jack of all trades may excel in adaptability and versatility, there's a risk of not attaining the depth of expertise necessary to truly master a craft. Yet, in its essence, this saying invites us to contemplate the balance between breadth and depth in our pursuits, encouraging us to embrace our multifaceted nature while also striving for excellence in our chosen domains.

Certainly! The adage "Jack of all trades, master of none" reflects the timeless debate surrounding the merits of specialization versus versatility.

People find their passion at an early age or maybe later which they work upon and turn it into a complete profession whereas there are also sorts of people who like to diversify their knowledge in different fields.

It suggests that individuals who possess a diverse range of skills, or who are able to adapt to various tasks and situations, may lack the depth of expertise found in those who focus solely on mastering a single craft or field.

It is fascinating in earlier times to see ourselves grow in different fields that are not interlinked to each other.

It's very rare to see them successful. The allure of being a jack of all trades lies in the flexibility and adaptability it offers. Such individuals are often seen as resourceful, capable, and diversified in handling a variety of challenges and tasks with relative ease.

They maintain different things at a time which makes them masters of management which is the ultimate requirement for anyone. They may thrive in dynamic environments where quick thinking and versatility are valued.

However, there's a risk that spreading oneself too thin across multiple interests or pursuits can lead to a lack of mastery in any one area. This happens due to a lack of focus. If a person is focusing on a lot of things in life, he/she at a point in time becomes blank. Without dedicating the time and effort required to achieve deep expertise, one may struggle to reach the pinnacle of success in a particular field.

Conversely, the pursuit of mastery in a specific domain demands focused attention, dedication, determination, time, effort, and often years of deliberate practice. Then the man finds his success, but what's the guarantee? I firmly believe with this point that to achieve anything in this life people require effort and discipline, but does it really make them successful? I doubt! I have also seen people putting effort into climbing a tree without legs but! Those who choose this path prioritize depth over breadth, immersing themselves fully in their chosen field to unlock its secrets and intricacies. While this approach may lead to unparalleled expertise and recognition, it may also come at the cost of versatility and adaptability in other areas.

Here destiny plays an important role as well as success or failure, nothing is in our hands and nothing is permanent. We just have to do actions that are moral and let God decide what to give based on our cycles.

We have to believe in time. Superior people prioritize their time more than anything. We have to understand that success or failure are not on our side neither on the other. It's just the right time which settle down all the subjects co-related to life.

Ultimately, the saying invites us to reflect on our own approach to learning and skill development. It prompts us to consider the trade-offs involved in pursuing breadth versus depth and encourages us to strike a balance that aligns with our goals and aspirations.

Whether we choose to be a jack of all trades or strive for mastery in a specific domain, the key lies in understanding our strengths, interests, and values, and charting a course that allows us to flourish in our own unique way.

Believe in time and God that's it!

2.
Multilateral > Unilateral

I am not here to create any debate and provoke. There are two kinds of people in this world:

1. Multilateral People

2. Unilateral People

Unilateral People are the kind of people who are extremely focused, determined, and disciplined and invest their time and energy in only one thing or subject that they love and are passionate about. Either they chose this path by themselves or were made to choose this path. There is nothing wrong with this personality in general. It is believed that this kind of people achieve success more than anyone and even more than multilateral ones. It's only dependent on the point of view of that person whether he/she loves or is passionate about their work or doing it with zero interest in it. Results clearly speak out.

Whereas, Multilateral Minds to which I belong are the kind of people who are not focused, determined, and disciplined on one single topic. They like to put their eggs in different baskets. They believe in diversification rather than just becoming a bee around honey. This multilateral mindset either comes from born talent or circumstances make them multitalented.

Is becoming a multi-dimensional WRONG?

Absolutely Not:)

Benefits of Being a Unilateral Mind:

- Focus
- Purpose

- Clear Goals
- No confusion and complexity
- Speed and Efficient

Unilateral people are clear and live with clarity. They have a clear purpose in life. They have an ambition and set small goals to achieve success. They work effectively and efficiently. Having one dream or goal allows a person to divert his/her abilities to one thing. They prefer not to be distracted by other topics.

Benefits of Multilateral Minds:

- Management
- Wider opportunities
- Diversified
- Creativity
- Adaptability

Multilateral people are diversified. Their knowledge and grip on different subjects might not be perfect but have vast understanding. This helps them to manage different things, especially time. The people who get a lot of extra time tend to participate in extra activities. Knowledge in different fields, helps them to get wider opportunities and build passive income sources. Multilateral people can easily grasp things that may be difficult for others but easy for them. They can adapt to different fields, areas of work, interests, work cultures, and different things.

There is always a question of whether one should learn in-depth in one's chosen field or should be an all-rounder. Should he/she be a 'Jack of all and a master of none'? Does it really help?

All around, multifaced persons are generally noticed and they climb up the ladder quickly as well. How and why does this happen?

Coming back to the question of advantages of being an all-rounder, it helps in:

1. **Making Friends–** As you have different topics to discuss, there are always people with whom you can strike up a conversation and continue it to a meaningful discussion. It helps to add depth to existing friendships. Multilateral people have quite a knowledge of every subject that exists and they are very good at making connections and relations with others. If you go near a multifaced guy and bring on a topic in front of him, he will either try to reply or at least step into that and gather information.

2. **Expanding Networks–** A network is the ultimate net worth. Rich and successful people understand this very well. How many people do you meet and exchange energies, thoughts, and knowledge that boost one's confidence? Multilateral people are so good at gathering a piece of information in any way possible. Because of the various interests, one friend will refer you to another friend and another will refer to some other, thereby increasing the network. You also have an opportunity to have a conversation in the various forums you meet.

3. **Group Members–** The people who have good genes which even include leadership and communication are a true blessing. In today's generation, parents prefer to have a single child which means that it needs to be specifically taught how to be part of a group activity and how as a group you always deliver higher results as compared to lone performers. Well Rounded as a Person helps to be a group person rather than a lone wolf. This quality is very sought after in most of the areas in the industry today. The guy who has great communication skills can lead a better life.

4. **Being Creative–** Creativity is everyone's subconscious brain; one has to just unlock it. Multilateral people are always busy with their lives in doing some or the other thing. Participating in some or the other events, activities, and others will increase the power and clarity. That person sometimes discovers the creative powers and creates wonders. For example, nowadays in IITs, theatre is one of the classes being mandated. How does that help? It helps to creatively think about different ways of solving the same problem. It gives a different perspective

5. **Reducing Dependencies–** Be it managing personal or professional setups, you have the confidence to make it happen when people are not around due to any sort of emergency. A very good example may be a dependency on a maid a cook or a person to generate reports for you. These are small things to learn but if you know to do it yourself, then dependencies can be a lot more reduced. Silence is good for peace of mind, but exposure can bring in more cheers. Multilaterals

are active around the clock! It's just their ability to always do something in their life.

6. **Broaden Knowledge–** As the individual has basic knowledge of varied things, he will able to quickly grasp the nuances and expand his knowledge. We tend to see quite many times that difficult to difficult topics are unable to be collected by unilateral or some kind of experts. But that difficult topic becomes a cakewalk for multilateral minds. They are so involved in everything that it doesn't take much time to grasp things.

7. **Find New Interests–** You get an opportunity to learn new things which might become the future passion/ part of research work/ Career opportunity. Multilateral minds are blessed with the ability to seek the right opportunities at the right time. They make things clear for themselves about what to do next in life. They make things ready and try to work for them.

8. **Release Stress–** Is it not common to see people burned down because of too much focus only in a certain area? Varied interests will help you relieve your stress, look out for options in other areas if required. I firmly believe that people who are extremely focused on one thing will achieve huge heights in their careers. Results may come earlier or later but it becomes worth it. Whereas multilateral-minded people have things to do, passion, profession, hobbies, interests, and stress busters as well.

9. **Develop Leadership Skills–** Leadership qualities come in a person at birth. I believe in this statement. Leadership and managing a team are only possible for people who are proficient in speaking. Leadership comes either through birth or through experience. At any given point in time, there will be areas where you want people to drive from the front and because you are multi-skilled, there will be plenty of opportunities to showcase and improve your leadership qualities. Multilateral people create a sensible personality.

10. **Shaping Your Personality–** You learn how to be more flexible, multi-talented, adaptable, and multi-tasker, gain discipline, and learn how to manage your time and ability to quickly learn new things that are sought after in any environment. Responsibility, resilience, and resourcefulness will help build your personality better. Management is a reward multilateral people get as they do all the work that may not make them masters of any but makes them masters of time and management. One's if a person knows how to control time, he will start controlling the world.

11. **Wholesome (End to End) Perspective–** Even in the IT industry, instead of just being a developer, tester, PM, or architect, having an appetite to learn other areas of work will help. In colleges and schools' management encourages students to participate in creative stuff and extra or co-curricular activities. As you grow up the ladder, all this information will be very handy and you will be able to better appreciate the problem at hand. Increasingly there is a blurring of

the boundaries between positions and flexibility is a much sought-after attribute in an employee. Talented all-rounders also can multi-task.

12. Improves Job Prospects– With agencies running lean in the current economic climate they are looking for talented individuals who have skills outside of the job description. Creative all-rounders definitely have the edge over those stuck in a rigid definition of their role, which is why it is important to be an all-round talent. Being an all-around talent is not just beneficial to your employer. It can mean a much more exciting and varied career if you have the skills and flexibility to move between roles. Be open to opportunities that are not necessarily in your job description; it can take you on an adventure that could be a great deal more rewarding than remaining rigidly in your role. Multilateral people suit for entrepreneurship. Entrepreneur has to have at least a basic touch of ideas in every field.

Being an all-rounder helps. The best position to be in would be to have 1 chosen field where you have a good depth and 3 to 4 allied streams.

3.
Diversify or die!

In this chapter, I would like to talk about personalities. There are a total 6 personalities in humankind like

- Alpha
- Sigma
- Beta
- Gamma
- Delta
- Omega

ALPHA PERSONALITY:

Alpha's we all know them. They are born leaders, achievers, focused, confident, competitive, dominant, and believe more in active sources and invest their time, money, and soul into it. The majority of the business tycoons, politicians, and many others have alpha traits in themselves. According to Harvard University, 70% of the world's top company senior executives are alpha males.

SIGMA PERSONALITY:

Sigma male is the most popular and common dream trait for majority of the teenagers. Sigma personalities are often described as lone wolves. They do not fit into traditional social hierarchies but still exhibit strong leadership traits in their own unique way. They are independent, self-sufficient, introspective, rebellious, and mysterious.

BETA PERSONALITY:

Beta-male personalities are often characterized as more submissive and supportive compared to alphas. They are cordial, reserved, loyal, dependent, and supportive.

Delta personalities are often described as the silent and withdrawn type. They tend to be more introverted and reserved compared to the other types. They are introverted, resilient, practical, realistic, observant and self-reliant. They have a small group of peers.

OMEGA PERSONALITY:

Omega personalities are often described as eccentric and nonconformist. They do not fit into traditional social hierarchies and often march to the beat of their own drum. They are nonconformists, intellectual, indifferent, creative, individuality.

GAMMA PERSONALITY:

Gamma's Can Be Easily Described in a Statement:

"Jack of all trades is a master of none

But oftentimes better than a master of one".

Gamma personality is a combination of all the personalities. Alpha + Sigma + Beta + Delta + Omega = Gamma.

Gamma isn't a master in all but has in-depth knowledge and experience in all the subjects they keep their feet in. Gamma personalities are often characterized as industrious and ambitious, but not necessarily dominant like alphas. They are mature versions of alphas. They are hard-working, ambitious, modest, creative, independent, respected, adaptable and reliable.

I have spoken a lot about gamma personalities because I am a gamma male, ha-ha.

Being a gamma, I relate to all the qualities above mentioned. I basically have mood swings most of the time. My thoughts and brain just wander all day. I am influenced heftily by mercury. Mercury is a planet and material.

Mercury is the fastest-moving planet compared to all the other planets. People who are influenced by mercury are not present at the moment at all. My brain doesn't stop raining ideas. I just have cyclones, tornadoes, earthquakes, collisions, and tectonic plates.

Ha ha, I am just kidding. According to Roman mythology, mercury has an incredible shape and is able to fly as fast as a bird. It completes its rotation around the sun in just 59 days. It travels at a speed of 29 miles per second which is 47 kilometers per hour.

Mercury as a material also doesn't have a shape. If it is kept in a glass, it becomes a glass shape. If it is kept in a bowl it takes out bowl shape. It becomes a colorless, odorless gas. It has the highest volatility compared to any metal.

The qualities that I mentioned above of mercury planet as well as material, does it sound great? Think!

Listen, every person has two faces One is shown and known and the other is unknown. Just the same every coin has two sides heads and tails, and probability is calculated on it.

According to Booker Talia ferro Washington, a leading African American intellectual of the 19th century. He says in one of his works names "Two Sides of Life". He mentions that there two sides even for life, one is the bright side and the other one is the dark side. People get confused with it. They fail to recognize the difference between the bright side and the dark side. This is the harsh truth, and live in such a stereotypical world with complex complicated minds.

Let me spit some facts, okay?

You have heard everything bad and the little dark part of the mercury, right? But mercury is considered the prince of all the planets. He has charisma and an elegant persona. Mercury in India is called out to be Budh. Budh's character describes four main sections:

- **Buddhi:** People with the influence of Budh attain Buddhi and knowledge on various subjects. May not become masters of them but attain an immense level of maturity at a young age.

- **Business:** In most parts of India and even in mythology merchants and businessmen pray to Budh to gain profits. As B for Budh, B for Business.

- On a Religious aspect mercury or Budh Graha is closest to Lord Vishnu amongst all the navagraha's in the system. Even in the past part of history when there is some Abhishekam (Bathing with some important materials from nature) to gods, goddesses, and even kings and queens. Each part of the abhishekam(Sacred Bath) builds power to different grahas.

Budh is necessary for growth and prosperity. It runs anything budh is important.

- **Buddhu:** Buddhu means illogical and idiotic sometimes. People call buddhu to someone when they behave or speak something that doesn't have a land and a roof.

This applies to Mercury Planet and I believe I spoke on both sides.

Now if we consider mercury material, what do you say/see? Colourless, Shapeless, Formless, and Odourless. Right?

According to Bruce Lee where he once described the character of water. "Empty our mind; be formless, shapeless, colourless, odourless just like water. Now you put water into a cup, it becomes a cup. If you put water in a bottle, it becomes a bottle. You put it into a teapot, it becomes the teapot. Now water can flow or it can crash. Be water, my friend".

It's such a heavy message given by a legend. Now some people consider themselves the high IQ ones. Will question me, hey Karthik you gave us a hefty essay on mercury speaking on its both sides and now giving us an example of water. Water = Mercury? What? You must have/had this question in your mind, right?

This is why we are lagging. People expect others to give them the best advice/solution/idea/thought my head my tail, but the actual reality is they aren't perfect at anything! They are just unsatisfied souls.

The basic idea mine taking the example of a legend is WATER. Bruce Lee Described and gave the best definition of water that nobody has given in the past present and future. It's just so perfect that it gives us the biggest life lesson.

"Just Like the Water, Just Go with The Flow."

I have been speaking a lot about IQ as well right. It is generally seen people with higher IQ's will be either become master of all or multitalented, excelling in whatever they choose because it's their interest. Even me I am not flexing but whatever somethings I have achieved in my life is all visualizing big things and out of the box stuff. It is surprising to me and my parents as well. I feel motivated, confident and superior to others all the time. I feel I am no less than anyone. But whether I am superior or not It doesn't matter. There is someone sitting at top who will settle all our scores.

4.
Don't Put All Your Eggs in One Basket

We shall now discuss about passive mindset. There are two types of voices one is active and the other one is passive. There are two types of incomes one is active and the other one is passive.

In the above-given statements in active and passive voice, in active voice, only two parties are talking to each other. Whereas in passive voice there are more than two parties in the conversation. In perspective of income, there are two as well active and passive. In terms of active income, a person is solely dependent on just one income, which is either most sufficient or insufficient. We tend to see people speaking and promoting active income but nobody does it. Everyone fakes it. Here we have passive income.

People nowadays are becoming financially literates and applying it in their lives, including me. People are making passive sources of income. They try to create income sources of more than 5.

Few people even manage 10 or more sources of income. Even if one gets closed or removed there is no burden because of the free flow of the income stream.

Whereas compared to an active source of income, if it is closed or terminated it's done. There is nothing left behind.

If you see in my case I have more than 5 sources of income at the age of 17 while I am writing this book. Owning an SMMA Agency (Social Media Marketing), Content Creation, Equities, Mutual funds, Derivatives, and now it is this book that will open a new gate of income source. It is what it is, I do! It is expected from a multilateral mind doing passive Income. I do it and appreciate everyone doing it.

Just the same we have active and passive mindsets. An active mindset is something that is just focused on something. The people who have an active mindset only invest their time, soul, and money into it. Whether the result favours them or not. Consistent efforts and discipline are put into it.

Whereas passive mindset, mine. People like me. We have different sources of paths to walk in. They didn't put their entire eggs in one basket but put their legs in different boats.

Is this a blessing or a curse? I firmly believe that I am blessed to have attained immense knowledge and expertise at a very young age. Which I don't see in my surroundings and peers.

From the early days of my childhood, I was always treated special and felt that I was different and not like others. I have been a victim of Buri Nazar (Evil Eye) since childhood. People, parents, and friends couldn't digest my success. I increased my spirituality and religious works.

Balancing myself with good self-control. People always call and tell me that I don't do work which suits my age. I have grown like a mature kid and I was always way ahead of my time.

Writing stories with no connection to surroundings, investing at a very young age, trading, writing songs, astrology, freelancing, Shayari's and poetry, music composition, piano, inter level swimming gold medallist, content creation, dance, singing and I don't even remember what I have done and doing currently.

I have countable friends. I pick just selected people and sit with them, but have healthy relations with all. I point out behavioural patterns, if they change, I change them. I have a good relationship with the seniors of my father's age. I don't play games and don't invest my time in things that gives me comfort or pleasure. I attend meetings, maintain connections, and efficient networking.

I don't have chit-chat with my friends or agemates, because they are interested in anime, games, and unwanted stuff in which I lack interest. I have chit-chat with the dads of my age mates regarding business news, equity markets scenarios, good stocks, suggestions, and many more.

I believe in the words of Mark Cuban, an American businessman, film producer, investor, and television personality. He is the former principal owner and current minority owner of the Dallas Mavericks of the National Basketball Association (NBA), co-owner of 2929 Entertainment, and one of the main "sharks" on the ABC reality television series Shark Tank.

Once he was invited to Oxford Union for an interview. A lady sitting in the audience questions him about the concept of portfolio careers. Because he is into media, sports, collaborating with entrepreneurs, and doing whatnot. She says that if she works for a little more time, she gets exhausted and witnesses Mark as he is doing plenty of stuff and achieving excellence in it.

Mark responds by saying that, He follows an overriding principle whether he likes it or not, is he having fun or not? He says that he is the luckiest guy in the world. He points out something interesting if he is having fun with this work or whatever is he doing, then something is wrong. He gets to do what he likes and people in this world are busy cursing their jobs. He mentions you come and you have to find the things that you like to do.

According to him the key to success is the work he likes to do and trying to be great at it. You don't have to know what that is. It's all about experimenting. It said that he took one computer class in college and cheated on it. When he started liking it poured his all interest into it.

Teaching himself programming and computer stuff for 20 hours a day and the days just go off. Because he loved it. He tried a lot of different things and only picked on what he liked to do. You just don't have to know what you want to be when you grow up. You just have to try different things even if 99% of it fails you will only be right one time.

You don't have to figure it all out in advance. You can be wrong, you can pick the wrong career, you can pick the wrong job, you can pick the wrong spouse, and wrong whatever. But you get right one time, you stand. But if you don't try, if you don't go out and try all these different things you will never get that one time. It doesn't mean how different things that I do and you should try, leave it. Try all of them until you like something. It gets really easy. Then it is a matter of consistency.

Let me tell some names of the historic legends who were multitalented and achieved immense respect and reputation.

1. **Leonardo-Da-Vinci (1452-1519):** He was a Painter, Architect, Engineer, Theatrical Producer, Scientist, Theorist, Sculptor, Humanist, Philosopher and Astronomer. He was considered as a universal genius by many.

2. **Alexander Porfiryevich Borodin (1833-1887):** He was a Musician, Music Composer, Scientist, Doctor, Chemist and Educationist.

3. **Michelangelo Buonarroti (1475-1564):** He was an Architect, Painter, Sculptor, Poet and Writer.

4. **Marcus Tullius Cicero (106BC-43BC):** He was a Humanist, Lawyer, Linguist, Orator, Philosopher, Politician and prose Stylist.

5. **Benjamin Franklin (1706-1790):** Founding Father of the United States. He has a wide range of interests including Natural Sciences, Literature, Politics, Inventor, Civil Activist, American Polymath, Printer, Statesman, Leading Writer, Diplomat, Author, and Political Theorist.

6. **Galileo Galilei (1564-1642):** He was most interested in Astronomy, Mathematics, Physics, Philosophy, Music and Art. He observed mountains on the moon, the Moons of Jupiter, Phases of Venus and Rings of Saturn.

7. **Robert Hooke (1643-1727):** He was an experimental Scientist, English Polymath, Astronomer, Physicist, Geologist, Meteorologist, Architect, Natural Philosopher, Mathematician and Surveyor.

8. **Issac Newton (1643-1727):** He was a Mathematician, Physicist, Astronomer, Theologian, Author, Alchemist and Natural Philosopher. Who doesn't know him?

9. **Johann Wolfgang Von Goethe:** He was a Poet, Novelist, Playwriter, Scientist and Philosopher.

10. **Abraham Lincoln:** He was the 16th President of The United States, Lawyer, Politician, Political Philosopher, and American Statesman.

11. **Aristotle:** He was a Philosopher, Musician, Polymath, Meteorologist, Metaphysics and Geologist.

12. **Rabindranath Tagore (1861-1941):** He was a Poet, Dramatist, Linguist, Grammarian, Educationist, Writer, Playwriter, Composer, Philosopher, Humanist, Universalist, Internationalist, Social Reformer, Painter, First Non-European and First Lyricist to get Noble Prize in Literature. Composer of the National Anthem of India. He Painted more than 2500+ paintings, wrote near to 2300 songs and what not.

13. **Chanakya (375-283 BCE):** He was a great Teacher, Indian Polymath, Author, Strategist, Philosopher, Economist, Jurist, Politician and Advisor of Chandragupta Maurya.

So on and so forth. Here If you observe something the the people whom I mentioned above didn't achieve success in all the things that they put their legs in. It's only one thing that made them popular. For Example, Leonardo-Da-Vinci. He did everything. From Astronomy to Philosophy, From Producer to Sculptor, From Humanist to Scientist, and whatnot but today people only recognize him for the Mona Lisa Art that he made. Did it take just a few days, no. It took him 16 years to make this masterpiece. It is only the interest, efforts and time you keep on something.

Here I have only mentioned the names of multitalented people. We find people around us either unilateral or multilateral who go unrecognized and unknown. Here in history, we have few noticed achievers. There are many more who are unknown due to various issues.

People go unnoticed due to social pressure, Parental Pressure, Bad Parenting, Lack of Motivation, Lack of Opportunities, Opportunities go unnoticed, Lack of Awareness, Depressed Past, Wrong Peer Group, and Not Believing in Time and God. Not one not two there are numerous issues with this society.

I am not promoting or demoting anyone or anything. It's just so miserable and devastating moment. People go on guilty for not doing something in the past. People underestimate themselves.

They think they are not worthy enough, and again people who are below average of them do big things. It's a message for everyone reading this. Notice, Appreciate and Encourage people around you who are doing something different to this so-called society.

The names that I mentioned above have huge respect from my side. Because you know unilateral and multilateral it its. Achieving something big with immense motivation and dedication on just one single thing, Is there any guarantee of success?

I don't believe it. Believe it or not but there is an influence and impact of TIME, LUCK, MONEY, ENERGY, and more in our lives. Everyone is equal but it doesn't mean that everyone has the same destiny, life, circumstances, money, thoughts, parents, spouse, kids, inner talents, and many more.

I respect the people whom I mention because they might not be the master of one, but let me tell you they are far better than the master of one. Either you put all your efforts into one single thing and expect it to give you bread and butter is a cruel thing according to me.

I believe in diversification just like the people above. Few so called intellectuals say that "Diversification is for COWARDS". Ha Ha I laugh at them.

Listen this world is FAKE! People are fake, Society is fake, Friends are fake, Relatives are fake, Smile is fake, Relations are fake, everything is just fake, fake, fake, fake. I'm sorry!

Everyone is just acting, everyone has 2 faces, The beautiful world that you are seeing has two faces it's absolute faeces.

I realized this thing in my childhood itself, I am the happiest. Yes, I am fake too like everyone else. I have issues to work on, problems unavoidable. But still I'm doing something.

This is the harsh reality. Listen as early you realise this you are safe. Believe in yourself, believe in God and breathe it will take you to the deepest breadth.

The beautiful world that you are seeing it isn't real and that pretty. Close your eyes and bring out a new light, that is success for me. If a snake isn't doing anything, be cautions it is about to do something.

The main point I am trying to explain is that, just don't take anything to seriously.

Listen to everyone, analyse and take your call. Do whatever possible in this mankind. I you feel it's correct, the god is happy Do it! I am doing the same thing as well.

I meditate on God, I talk to God, God is everything. If I am not doing something right, I get a wakeup call from God directly. Maintain that connection with him/her. It's the most precious one that you can afford for. Escape from this blind route, follow your passion.

5.
Pick Passive

Pick Passive

One of the Prime Minister's financial advisors once attended a podcast on YouTube discussing about Economics and addressing important policies and practices.

He mentions about the Unilateral and Multilateral view of the entire nation, economies and markets. By listening to his perspective, I made my mind clear that there are also people like me who PICK PASSIVE.

He addresses an issue with the country named Cuba, officially the Republic of Cuba is an island country. Cuba is located where the northern Caribbean Sea, Gulf of Mexico, and Atlantic Ocean meet. Cuba is the third-most populous country in the Caribbean after Haiti and the Dominican Republic, with about 11 million inhabitants. It is the largest country in the Caribbean by area.

According to a 2022 report from the Cuban Human Rights Observatory (OCDH), 72 percent of Cubans live below the poverty line. 21 percent of Cubans who live below the poverty line frequently go without breakfast, lunch or dinner due to a lack of money. Pensions are among the smallest in the Americas at $9.50/month.

Due to the past struggles this country widely invests in Health sector. Is it the number one health hub, no. But yeah, this country has one of the highest literacy rates in the world.

There are countries which are having inheritant natural resources or the special advantages is a boon for the economy, right? But no.

It is seen that countries with their natural resources with become rich but not developed. This happens due n number reasons.

If you just invest in one single thing, you will not be able to. Are there any guarantee of success or fancy aims that we keep in our mind? In terms of nations, if you have a unilateral perspective and promote one single thing you will end up not being a successful country.

It even applies to nature. If you only have tigers, they starve and die. If you only have goats, they starve and die. If you only have plants, then what's the use. There is something called ECOSYSTEM. Things in our universe are like connected dots. Everything is connected and interlinked with each other.

What is Economics? You cannot Invest in one single thing.

This is economics in one sentence. Health will argue it is important, Education will argue it is important, Transport will argue it is important, Infrastructure will argue it is important, but at the end what is important. It is one single thing which connects all these things and that is Economics I simply mean budget allocated for these different things. No budget no functioning. Right!

Same with a cricket team Batsmen will argue he is important, Bowler will argue he is important, Wicket-Keeper will argue it is important, Fielder will argue he is important but at the end what is important? The collective efforts of each sector contribute towards the success of a TEAM. To run a team, you need everything. Captain, Vice-Captain, Coaches, Board Member, Sponsor's and many others. Right!

In case of Human Body. Eyes will argue it is important, Legs will argue it is important, Hands will argue it is important, Mind will argue it is important, but at the end what is important? It's the same question that I have asked.

The collective efforts and circulation of each body parts will result to the functioning of Human Body. Right!

Now people will argue with me. Hey Karthik, you started with Multilateral Mind and why are you coming to all these things.

Simply said. It's not about the Governments, People, Cricket Team, and others. At the end it is Team Work.

"Co-operation, Co-ordination and Collaboration, 3C's for Success" according to me.

6.
Mind Management

There are two kinds of people, one is RICH and the other one is WEALTHY. Rich and Wealthy hear same but different.

To take an example, there is Elon Musk. We all know him right. Founder, CEO, and chief engineer of SpaceX

CEO and product architect of Tesla, Inc.

Owner, CTO and Executive Chairman of X (formerly Twitter)

President of the Musk Foundation

Founder of The Boring Company, X Corp., and xAI

Co-founder of Neuralink, OpenAI, Zip2, and X.com (part of PayPal)

Is he Rich or Wealthy?

Rich obviously right, but why not wealthy. See I do admire his work and achievements and I am no one to justify what he is doing. But I don't take him as an Idol. Because he might be the world richest person but failed as a husband thrice, failed as a father what he did is only work. Obviously, the amount of work that he is dealing with is huge but it effects relationships. But yeah, his futuristic and out of the box thinking gave us the greatest results. He is a Legend.

Well, this book isn't him, he is not WEALTHY. To become wealthy a person has to first master BALANCE.

- Spiritual
- Financial
- Social

- Physical
- Emotional

Nobody in this world at a time can master these things not even God. But managing it and balancing will make a person Wealthy. Spiritual wellbeing is for mind refreshment and mind management.

If you are Financially fit, life becomes lit. social networking maintaining and managing relationships. Physical Wellbeing will make a person physically fit and generates energy. Emotional wellbeing is necessary to achieve anything in life. Thus, we have to learn it ourself cause no school is going to teach this. Renaissance period is over but we have to adopt such great living standards to achieve anything.

I want to do everything the idea of being pushed into this box and deprived of the room to Branch out and try different things that's horrible to me and chances are this get even worse when you enter a career because of this hyper specialized economy we've built that's not how humans work we're on this Earth for more than being just a cog in a machine doing this one specific task and becoming good at one specific thing.

If you share the same feeling that's amazing because that becomes a part of a person who is curious and a lifelong learner.

I am one of them who is always wanting to try new things and explore everything. This feeling is great but dangerous if not not managed properly.

In the chase of doing everything you end up nowhere. Jack of all trades master of none – this requires balance. If we just jump from hobby to hobby, interest to interest and business to business, it's not going to work.

I myself invested a little amount of time in each hobby and interest never expecting any success. But later realised that my surroundings and the life that I am living is filled with ideologies of success. I never succeeded in the traditional way that everyone wants.

I like the idea of a renaissance man. A Renaissance man does everything, the people are extremely multitalented, fit healthy and wealthy. But the time that I am living in, is not a renaissance age. I live in the era where you keep success aside, participating this huge competition is a big thing. We have to be generalist but never lose our interest.

Doing everything is next to impossible. We are humans not machines. With growing age our responsibilities grow as well.

Thus, creativity and curiosity inside us dies. If you are attending an event, it's obvious that you would want to taste everything you see. You fill your plate completely, but your body has some limits and can't digest it all.

- For that we have to first Plan and Budget our time because it's the same, everybody has the same 24 hours a day and 7 days a week. Plan and jot down all the ideas, hobbies, interests, requirements, wants and needs. Narrowing all the things and make a final checklist and budget our time for that. Because planning our all works on how important they are will provide us clarity and vision.

- **Time Management:** If you are the master of time management, you can literally do anything. Time Management is the same repeated thing everywhere. You see it in self-help books, speeches and just everywhere. But it works. Billionaire and most successful people value their time more than money. They invested their time on the right thing and now money is chasing them.

Spending time only with one single thing is wrong again. If you only study, you might become a topper but you will lack communication and other things. If you only work, work, work your relationships might fail. Balance is necessary.

- **Combine Activities:** Multitasking is great and achievable. Do two things which complement each other. You can listen to podcasts or audiobooks while exercising. You can take important calls while cooking, walking or doing some work. Mind can't put effort on two things together, for that we have to do one thing which requires attention and simultaneously do the other which doesn't require attention.

- **Quality over Quantity:** Instead of doing all the things in a day. We should schedule our works. Doing all the things in a day and using ultimate potential ability of ours will not work. Comfortably we can do things for couple of days but with time it will fail.

So, just minimise tasks for every day. If you achieve it, treat yourself. If you treat your mind well it is going to work well for you.

- **Diminishing Marginal Utility:** This is that one life lesson that I learnt through my business. In the starting of my business when luckily, I starting getting clients. I was happy but again I wanted more. I tried my best and got few. But not sufficient again. This is a bad thing. Instead of just going on hitting the clients you fail to provide the quality service that you promised to give.

The Law of Diminishing Marginal Utility states that when a consumer goes on consuming a standard unit of a commodity, the additional utility in every successive unit of consumption keeps on diminishing. It is based on the assumption that the consumer needs to consume a standard unit of the commodity. This is an important chapter of Economics.

During my High School where I was taught this chapter, I understood it very well but only till the subject, not in the real life. I learnt this realising my mistakes in business and hobbies that I was inclined to.

I am suggesting it to you to not do the same. Successful people don't waste their time and energy wearing fancy clothes and dresses. It is the same set of clothes that they wear repeatedly.

So Yeah, Diversification is not wrong but managing and balancing should be taken with utmost care.

- The last one is Mood Swings. In today's generation there is too much of mood swings. There is just less attention span. Which is leading to quick early success and suddenly disappear.

While starting something new, it's always that motivation coming in. The things go well, productive work, you feel like you are just winning until that feeling pause.

Suddenly you feel your work is getting dead. No movement at all. You lose your hope and finally you decide to quit before you are about to get the success.

People today, they watch something. Not good they change, if good they watch more. People are having numerous options with them. This is good and bad. Bad because immense saturation and dilution for over competition. Good because it is easy to succeed. So just don't change your mood, just trust the process and go with the flow.

www.ingramcontent.com/pod-product-compliance
Lightning Source LLC
LaVergne TN
LVHW061622070526
838199LV00078B/7393